THE LITTLE BOOK OF DUBLIN

Tom Galvin graduated from UCD and St Patrick's College, Maynooth before leaving for Poland where he was based as a teacher with APSO, the state body for overseas development. There he began his career as a journalist with the *Warsaw Voice* and Radio Polonia, returning to Ireland in 2000 to work as a staff writer and later editor of *In Dublin* magazine. As a freelance journalist he has written for many newspapers, including the *Evening Herald* and *The Irish Times,* and as an eager travel writer for *Backpacker* and *Abroad* magazines.

THE LITTLE BOOK OF DUBLIN

Tom Galvin

NEW ISLAND

THE LITTLE BOOK OF DUBLIN
First published 2004
by New Island
2 Brookside
Dundrum Road
Dublin 14
www.newisland.ie

ISBN 1 904301 10 X

British Library Cataloguing in Publication Data. A CIP catalogue record for this book is available from the British Library.

Typeset by New Island
Cover design by New Island
Printed in Ireland by ColourBooks

10 9 8 7 6 5 4 3 2 1

CONTENTS

PAST
TO
THE
PRESENT

FROM HIGH KINGS
TO VIKINGS TO THE
VIRGIN MEGASTORE:
DUBLIN'S HISTORY AT
A GLANCE

What's in a name? With their building of numerous ring forts (*rath*) and forts (*dún*) in about 250 BC, the first Gaelic settlers of Dublin gave us such place-names as Rathfarnham, Rathmines and Dun Laoghaire. We can thank the Vikings for the names of Dublin's islands, as the Viking word for island (*ey*) formed the names Lamb Ey (Lambay Island), Dalk Ey (Dalkey Island) and Ireland's Ey (Ireland's Eye). And for the Dubliners' legendary intellect we can surely be grateful to a King Eystein, who reigned in the city between AD 873 and 875.

Gaelic Dublin originally consisted of two settlements: Áth Cliath (ford of the hurdles) and Dubh Linn (black pool), the former secular and the latter ecclesiastical. The black pool is believed to have been where the present-day gardens of Dublin Castle are located, the hurdle ford where Father Mathew Bridge now joins Church Street and Bridge Street. The word *baile* (town) was added to the secular settlement's name some time towards the end of the fourteenth century to give us the modern Irish name for Dublin: Baile Áth Cliath.

All roads lead to Dublin. The Áth Cliath settlement was where the four great roads of ancient Ireland met: the Slighe Midluachra from Ulster, the Slighe Mór from Connaught, the Slighe Chualann from South Leinster and the Slighe Dála from Munster. High standards were imposed, however. *Slighe* was defined as a road wide enough to allow two chariots to pass each other, as opposed to *bóthar*, a minor road that had to be only the width of two cows – one lengthways and one crossways.

The story behind the naming of Áth Cliath is an amusing one. A payment of one hundred and fifty ladies plus seven hundred white cows with red ears was demanded by Conall Carnach to avenge the death of his foster brother, Cúchulainn. Legend has it that the bridge of hurdles, composed of mats of branches, was laid across the River Liffey to allow this herd to cross. One can presume the women crossed the same way.

The original St Patrick's Cathedral was built in the fifth century on an island created where the River Poddle divided in two before joining the Liffey at the 'black pool'. A spot marked with a Celtic cross at the west end of the nave was where St Patrick baptised and converted the masses in about AD 450. He was also credited with producing three miraculous wells – one near the cathedral, another in the grounds of Trinity College and the third in Nassau Place. The well near the cathedral is said to be responsible for the success of Guinness.

The Vikings who began plundering the east coast in the eighth century came mostly from Norway and Denmark. The name of the town of Baldoyle, a large Viking settlement, comes from the Irish 'Baile Dubh

4

Ghaill' (the town of the dark foreigners). The name specifically refers to those Vikings who came from Denmark, known as *dubh ghaill* (black-haired foreigners), rather than the Vikings from Norway, who were termed *fionn ghaill* (white-haired foreigners) and from whom the name of Fingal County in north Dublin is derived.

Viking settlements were established by the construction of the 'Thingmote' (also known as a 'Thingmount') – an assembly place that consisted of a flat-topped hill about thirteen metres high where the king would sit. The Thingmote in Dublin stood near the present-day College Green but was levelled in 1681. When the earth from this structure was spread out on what is now Nassau Street, it raised the level of the road by eight feet, which explains the difference in levels now between Nassau Street and College Park.

The Vikings were the first to mint coins in Dublin, but it's unlikely these coins sparkled for long. Instead of carrying purses, they concealed their money by sticking the coins with beeswax to the hair under their armpits.

Vikings intermarried freely with the native Irish, whose behaviour in matrimonial matters can only be regarded as suspect. Brian Boru, King of Munster – who defeated the Vikings at Clontarf in 1014 – married Gormflaith, who was mother of King Sitric of Dublin and sister of Maolmordha, King of Leinster. King Sitric in turn married Brian Boru's daughter. Go figure.

The city walls of Dublin were raised by the Ostmen, or Danes, in the ninth century. However, in the twelfth century the exterior became more familiar to them when they were banished by the Anglo-Normans to an area that became known as Ostmanstown on the north side of the Liffey, a tag that survives in the locally named Oxmantown Road. From then on, the people who lived and worked within the medieval walls were considered to be of English blood.

What did the Normans ever do for us? Dublin expanded greatly in the years following the Norman capture of the city in 1170. Apart from building Dublin Castle, the Normans also built castles at Castleknock, Drimnagh, Dalkey and Clondalkin.

The Normans rebuilt Christ Church Cathedral, founded by the Viking King Sitric as the Church of the Holy Trinity, in 1172. St Patrick's Cathedral was rebuilt in 1192, modelled on Salisbury Cathedral in England.

The Normans fortified the city walls and built elaborate gateways at various points. St Audoen's Arch is the only surviving gateway. They diverted the River Poddle to run around the walls on the south and east; with the Liffey on the north side, the city then had a natural defence.

The Normans built the first real bridge over the Liffey (at the site of the present Father Mathew Bridge) in 1215, introduced rabbit into the country's diet and brought the first water supply to the city.

*B*urying our waste seems to be an age-old tradition in Dublin. In the fifty years of Norman domination, the quayside of the city was actually built upon large deposits of household waste and supported by a series of wooden fences. These fences were built on the riverside, and refuse was dumped behind them to reclaim land from the river itself.

The entrances to both of Dublin's medieval churches – Christ Church and St Patrick's Cathedral – lie below the present street level by some three metres, and the explanation lies in the build up of rubbish over time. The wooden houses of medieval Dublin would have lasted only a generation or two before being knocked down and new homes being built. Mounting refuse would have contributed to the rise in surface level.

Moving into the new millennium, by 2001 Dublin Corporation was collecting approximately 650 tonnes of rubbish every day.

*D*ublin Castle was built on the orders of King John, son of Henry II, in 1204, and the task was completed in 1230. Henry III, who never actually came to Ireland, ordered the construction of a great hall modelled on the one in Canterbury. Built between 1243 and 1245, it was the first building in Dublin to get a piped water supply.

While stray cats and dogs are a problem in most cities, in medieval Dublin the problem was stray pigs. The number of pigs roaming the streets was such that bailiffs were ordered to kill them with pikes and stack the carcasses on carts. Today, according to the Dublin Society for the Prevention of Cruelty to Animals, there are about three thousand horses in the Dublin city and county area living on the side of the road, on vacant lots or in back gardens.

Although held in some esteem by the Irish after Mel Gibson's 1995 film *Braveheart*, the Scottish king Robert Bruce caused havoc in Ireland. He came to the aid of his brother Edward after he had marched on Dublin in 1317 with an army of twenty thousand men, destroying everything in his path.

While the army camped at Castleknock, the citizens of Dublin panicked, and any structure that could aid an attack was torn down. St John's Hospital and the belfry of the Church of St Mary del Dam (where City Hall stands at present) were razed, four-fifths of the suburban area was set alight and part of Christ Church was destroyed. The Scots were so impressed with the Dubliners' resolve, they abandoned their attempt to capture the city.

Edward Bruce was later slain at Faughart, County Louth, in 1318, allowing the Anglo-Irish in Dublin to breathe a sigh of relief.

In 1454 (and again three years later, since it was possibly ignored the first time round), Dublin Corporation issued a decree informing all men and women of Irish blood to leave the city walls. The bulk of those evicted settled in Irishtown. 'Masterless' people (the unemployed, basically) were also forbidden to reside within the walls of the city.

Gradually, the Gaelic and Anglo-Norman elements settled down together, and by 1494, the only region to remain loyal to the Crown was Dublin and its immediate environs, an area roughly fifty kilometres long and thirty kilometres wide. This area was surrounded by a double ditch and became known as 'the Pale' (from the Latin word for 'stake'). Hence the expression 'beyond the pale', pertaining to a region deemed to be beyond control.

In 1512, a row broke out between two rivals, the Butlers, Earls of Ormond, and the Fitzgeralds, Earls of Kildare. During one clash, the Earl of Ormond fled and took refuge in the chapter-house of St Patrick's Cathedral, barricading himself behind the door. He refused to come out until his rivals promised he would not be harmed. To cement the assurance, Kildare's soldiers cut a hole in the door so Ormond could shake hands with his enemy. The expression 'to chance your arm' comes from this incident.

*I*n 1534, Dublin experienced Ireland's first recorded earthquake. But the greatest disaster in the city took place in Wood Quay (known as Coal Quay in the eighteenth century, owing to its proximity to the city coal yard).

On 11 March 1596, while a large quantity of gunpowder was being unloaded from a ship, the clerk in charge bunked off for a mug of ale. Children were seen rolling the barrels of gunpowder down the street, and a nail in one of the casks was said to have sparked, igniting the powder and causing an enormous explosion. In total, 126 people lost their lives. The force of the explosion was such that it cracked the bell in the tower of nearby Christ Church.

A ruling in 1661 forbade the use of thatch for roofing to prevent fires. Pity London hadn't done the same before the Great Fire ravaged the city in 1666. However, after that tragedy the citizens of Dublin contributed over a hundred thousand head of cattle to the people of London as a gesture of goodwill. The citizens of Dublin again came to the rescue of a neighbour in need when, in 1941, Dublin Fire Brigade rushed to the aid of Belfast in the aftermath of a German bombing.

*W*hy do the Irish talk incessantly about the weather? One reason may be subliminal messaging. During the seventeenth century, a town crier was employed to walk the streets of the city nightly at 10.00 p.m., midnight,

2.00 a.m. and 4.00 a.m. in winter and at 11.00 p.m., 1.00 a.m. and 3.00 a.m. in summer, giving the hour and the state of the weather at the time.

1n 1649, Cromwell arrived in Ringsend with twelve thousand troops, set to wreak havoc on the native Irish. However, we do have something to thank him for, since it was Oliver's Army that brought one of the staples of Irish food – cabbage – to the country for the first time. 'The Cabbage Patch', the Protestant graveyard that was established opposite St Patrick's Cathedral in 1668, was where cabbages were first planted by Cromwell's troops. It is now a public park.

The statue of King William that was erected in College Green in July 1701 was a constant target for vandals, mostly radical students from Trinity College who were said to have resented King Billy having his back turned to them. In 1710, two students were fined and jailed for six months for defacing the statue. In 1805, another student painted the statue black on the eve of the king's birthday, managing to persuade the watchman that he had been sent by the Corporation. In 1836, it was blown apart by a bomb, but the pieces were collected and the statue restored. When it was blown up again in 1929, the statue was finally abandoned. At that point, it had been reconstructed so many times that the raised left leg was about a foot longer than the right.

In 1737, Jonathan Swift published *A Proposal for Giving Badges to the Beggars in all Parishes of Dublin* – these would be metal badges identifying the beggar's parish so he or she could not beg outside it.

In 1729, Swift penned *A Modest Proposal for Preventing the Children of Poor People in Ireland from Being a Burthen to Their Parents, or Country, and for Making Them Beneficial to the Publick*, in which he stated, 'I have been assured by a very knowing American of my Acquaintance in London, that a young healthy Child well nursed, is at a Year old, a most delicious, nourishing, and wholesome Food, whether Stewed, Roasted, Baked or Boiled ...'

Swift, however, subscribed to the principle of living on one-third of his income, saving a third and donating a third to charity. His donations funded an asylum in Steeven's Lane.

*N*ewgate Gaol, originally situated between High Street and Thomas Street and forming part of the medieval New Gate, was established in 1285 under Richard II. Proving that corruption is not only a modern blight, in 1729 an enquiry found that warden John Hawkins, who was on an annual salary of £10, had actually amassed a total of £1,150 through bribery. To receive their staples of cell, food and drink, the inmates had had to pay handsomely. Otherwise, they were condemned to the cellars, stripped naked and beaten.

*B*artholomew Mosse, in 1745, opened the first maternity hospital in Ireland in George's Lane. He leased a house that had previously been owned by a celebrated 'rope dancer' and converted it into a twenty-four bed 'lying-in' hospital. Here, for almost twelve years, he put up the poorest women of Dublin until he raised funds to build a new hospital at Parnell Square, which later became known as the Rotunda Hospital. Four thousand and forty-nine children were born in Dr Mosse's hospital.

The man himself found his resting place in Donnybrook graveyard in 1759, a site on the main street that was originally an eighth-century convent. The graveyard is known as a place where only the graves of nonentities are identifiable. There is no clue as to the graves of any of the notables who are buried there.

In 1801, the Union Jack was first raised, not in England, but over Dublin Castle, on 1 January when the Act of Union came into effect and the Irish Parliament was abolished. The Act of Union was most damaging to Dublin City. The transfer of power to Westminster reduced the city to a regional capital, and its leading citizens, together with their money and influence, moved to London or the suburbs. They were then outside the jurisdiction of Dublin Corporation, which depended on them for taxes and the financial costs of supporting the city's workhouses, hospitals and police. Many buildings in salubrious areas, such as Mountjoy Square, Gardiner Street, Henrietta Street and Summerhill in the north city centre, became some of the worst slums in Europe.

The story of Dublin city in the nineteenth century is a story of the poor. The professional class accounted for only 7.6 per cent of the population in 1881. Samuel Foote, the English actor-satirist, said at the time that he had never known what London beggars did with their clothes until he saw Dublin beggars.

Nine Martello towers were built around Dublin at various points from 1804 as a defence against a possible Napoleonic attack. When the threat subsided, all the garrisons were disbanded, but the British War Office overlooked the one on Dalkey Island, the first residents on the island for hundreds of years. The garrison continued to be paid and remained there until late into the next century, when some died of old age and others eventually drifted off. The name Martello comes from Cape Martello in Corsica, where a similar type of tower resisted a British attack in 1794.

In 1818, the General Post Office (GPO) was opened, having been built for a fairly modest £50,000. It boasted statues on the pediment – Hibernia, representing Ireland, rested on her spear and harped shield, while the functions of the building were epitomised by Mercury and Fidelity. However, *Wakeman's Guide to Ireland* (1890) records a conversation between a tourist and a cab driver who was asked the meaning of the three figures. The cab driver glanced at the building and replied that it was the twelve apostles. When the tourist enquired as to the whereabouts of the other nine, the cab driver replied, 'With weather like this they only come out three at a time, takin' their turns regular.'

The tower of St Werburgh's Church in the upper yard of Dublin Castle, once one of the tallest towers in Dublin, was removed in the early nineteenth century because it was deemed to be a possible vantage-point for a sniper.

*H*e was not an Irishman, and he never visited the country in his life, but his remains managed to end up in Dublin. Who are we talking about? St Valentine, who is remembered world-wide on 14 February, lies beneath a side altar in Whitefriar Street Church. Pope Gregory XVI sent his remains as a gift to the Carmelite order in 1835.

*I*n the early nineteenth century, body-snatching became so prevalent that five watch-towers were built in Prospect Cemetery, Glasnevin, and guards patrolled the grounds with Cuban bloodhounds. Body-snatching was a popular pursuit, as even a full set of teeth at the time could fetch you a pound in a medical school. The Anatomy Act of 1832 put an end to the days of these 'resurrectionists', and the donation of bodies to medical science was legalised.

*I*n 1844, Dublin Zoo received its first giraffe and in 1855 bought its first pair of lions. Clearly a source of great 'pride' for the owners, the carnivorous animals kept their place at the top of the food chain at the expense of the other animals when food supplies dwindled during the Easter Rising, 1916. A stroke of good luck, some would say, because on 20 March 1927, Cairbre, the lion used to introduce Metro-Goldwyn-Meyer films, was born there.

*I*n the winter of 1847, during one of the worst periods of the Great Famine, the poor pleaded for scraps and the Lord Lieutenant, the Earl of Bessborough, ordered the cook in Dublin Castle to send out a beef bone for the communal stock-pot. He died not long afterwards, and as his body was being taken from the castle, the crowd taunted the cortège by dangling a bone from a pole.

*L*et them eat … soup? So many people flocked to Dublin in search of food during the Great Famine that workhouses were stretched to the limit. In 1847, the Soup Kitchen Act was passed, and soup stalls were set up to feed the multitudes.

A French chef, Alexis Soyer, was hired to prove his theory that a bowl of his distinctive soup and a piece of bread could last a man for a day. His magic recipe was ox head, corn, carrot, turnip, onion, cabbage, peas and leeks. His soup kitchen at Croppies Acre near Kingsbridge had a boiler that held three hundred gallons of soup, and people filed through a wooden hut forty feet long. One hundred clients could be served at a time.

By the middle of 1847, over three million people were receiving relief in the city.

*I*n 1862, the first fire brigade was established in Dublin at Whitehorse Yard off Winetavern Street. Before this, the responsibility for avoiding disaster was left to the insurance companies, which had to run their own fire brigades for whichever buildings happened to be on their books.

*D*ubliners were amused in 1907 when the crown jewels – known as the Regalia of the Order of St Patrick, a symbol of the unity between the Crown and the loyal landed gentry in Ireland – were stolen from the Bedford Tower of Dublin Castle under the noses of the police force. The theft was not discovered until the eve of the arrival of King Edward VII to open the International Exhibition at Ballsbridge. The culprit was never caught. Sir Arthur Vicars, the official guardian, was the scapegoat. However, he was convinced that the brother of Irish explorer Sir Ernest Shackleton was behind the theft.

*W*hen the GPO was taken over by the Volunteers during the 1916 Rising, windows were smashed to allow a line of fire, then barricaded with wax dummies from an exhibition in nearby Henry Street. Some of the statues that were shot at by the British forces included King George V, Queen Mary and Lord Kitchener.

The Irish Free State officially came into being on 6 December 1922, but not everyone embraced it. During the 1926 Horse Show at the Royal Dublin Society, the British jumping team was greeted with a chorus of 'God Save the King' and the Irish Army Team with silence. The Council of the Irish Rugby Union refused to fly the Irish tricolour and flew the Union Jack until 1932, when the Taoiseach, William Cosgrave, intervened.

In January 1941, German bombs fell on Terenure and Harold's Cross, and on 31 May 1941 several bombs fell on Dublin's North Strand, killing thirty-seven people. After the war, the British Air Ministry acknowledged that it had diverted the guide beam used by the Germans, who thought they had been over Britain at the time and not over neutral Ireland. By way of compensation, the Irish government was paid £327,000 in the 1950s – by the Germans.

In 1942, gas rationing was introduced in Dublin. Its use was restricted to certain hours of the day. But the shrewd Dubliners discovered that there was a 'glimmer' of gas left in the pipes once the supply was cut off – enough to boil a kettle during the forbidden hours. The Gas Company introduced an official to detect culprits, who became known in the city as the 'glimmerman'.

Limerick-born Michael Manning was the last man to be lawfully executed in Ireland. He went to the gallows in Mountjoy Jail on 20 April 1954 for the murder of an elderly nurse.

Both the sale and importation of condoms was banned in Ireland in 1935, but in February 1991, the ironically named Virgin Megastore on Aston Quay dared to ignore the ban and faced the wrath of the Irish Family Planning Association. The government promised a review but was stymied by the Catholic Church, warning of 'dire consequences' should the ban be lifted. Eventually, the purchase of condoms was permitted to anyone over the age of seventeen.

Dr Dermot Ryan, the Archbishop of Dublin in November 1972, was the first Catholic bishop since the Reformation to attend a service in Christ Church Cathedral.

In December 1997, President Mary McAleese, just two months into her term, caused a storm by accepting communion at a Church of Ireland ceremony in St Patrick's Cathedral.

THE
CITY

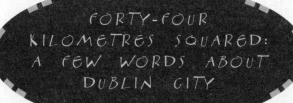

FORTY-FOUR
KILOMETRES SQUARED:
A FEW WORDS ABOUT
DUBLIN CITY

*D*ublin City covers an area of 44.4 square kilometres. From the westernmost point to the most easterly tip is a distance of 18.75 kilometres; north to south is 13.15 kilometres. In 2004, 495,101 people were living in this area.

Dublin is twinned with San Jose, California, USA (1986), Liverpool, England (1997) and Barcelona, Spain (1998).

There are twelve places called Dublin in the United States and six in Australia.

*T*he city's motto is somewhat totalitarian in its delivery: 'Obedientia Civium Urbis Felicitas' meaning 'The obedience of the citizens is the happiness of the city'. The armorials of the city of Dublin – three flaming castles – were confirmed and entered in 1607 but their origins remain a mystery. The city seal in 1229 had a castle on one side and a ship on the other, and in general, three figures were used to fill an armorial shield and to stress a symbol. It is possible that the flaming castle portrays the defence of Dublin from the attacks of the Irish from the Wicklow mountains.

*T*he celebration of Dublin's own millennium in 1988 was entirely dubious, since the city as an urban settlement goes back a lot further than a thousand years. In 989 (we got it slightly wrong because dates prior to 1014 in the Annals were incorrect by one year), High King Máel Sechnaill II captured Dublin for a second time and, on this occasion, exacted tribute by way of a tax on the Norse population, thereby claiming the city as belonging to Ireland. As the annalist put it, 'he captures the town and makes it Irish'.

In 2000, 6.4 million people visited Dublin, spending a total of €2,647 million. The most popular month to visit that year was August, with a figure of 286,437 walk-in customers to the city's main tourist offices. The most popular tourist attraction proved to be the National Gallery of Ireland; the least visited attraction was Balbriggan Castle.

The greatest complaint from visitors to the capital is that they were robbed. Dublin is the third most expensive capital city in the EU, coming twenty-first in the world list in 2003, up from seventy-third in 2002.

Rain in Ireland is notorious, but Dubliners can count themselves lucky because they live in what is officially the driest city in the land. In 2000, 840.2 millimetres of rain fell, which, compared with the wettest day on record – 101.6 millimetres on 25 August 1905 – makes it barely a splash.

The average temperature for the coldest month in Dublin, January, stands at 4.8 Celsius/40.6 Fahrenheit; and for the hottest month, July, the average temperature is 15.0 Celsius/59.0 Fahrenheit.

In 1616, as part of the Candlelight Law, Dublin Corporation ordered that every fifth house should have a candle lit in the window as a form of public lighting. Fish-blubber fuel replaced candles by the end of the seventeenth century, and by 1825, gas lamps had appeared; they were replaced by electric lamps in 1892. In 1986, Dublin Corporation was allocated over £5 million for the upkeep of thirty-six thousand streetlights.

At the time of the 1991 census, over two-thirds of all housing in the city was less than fifty years old. Some 2,362 houses of various types were completed in Dublin in 2000, the largest proportion of these being apartments.

Prices for new houses in the city went from an average of £76,000 in 1996, to £174,000 in 2000 – an incredible 98 per cent increase.

In 2002, the number of private households in Dublin stood at 368,534, compared to 144,718 in Cork and 64,228 in Galway.

The average industrial wage in the city has not risen dramatically enough in recent years to help people cope with the rise in property prices. In 1996, the average wage was £14,748 and in 2001 it was £18,458. This is only a 25 per cent increase.

TRANSPORT

HORSES, TRAMS AND THE (JERRY LEE) LUAS: GETTING AROUND DUBLIN

Dublin City has 42.8 kilometres of National Primary Roads and 1,133 kilometres of non-national Roads. One can travel around Dublin by Dublin Bus or by Dublin Area Rapid Transit (DART). Dublin Bus carried 193 million passengers in 1997. The DART carries roughly ninety thousand passengers a day, compared with nine thousand a day on the previous diesel system.

From 1987, commuters on the DART enjoyed a spot of culture with the Poetry in Motion project displaying poems in the carriages in poster form – until 1996, when the poems briefly and quietly slipped away. Letters from irate commuters brought about their return under the title Poets' Corner: a poem is now posted in the corners of the carriages.

Ever wondered if there is a logic to the numbers on Dublin buses? They follow the system used in the days of the horse-drawn trams, which ran from the city centre outwards in a clockwise direction from south to north. So number 3 went to Sandymount, 7 to Blackrock, 10 to Donnybrook, 11 to Clonskeagh and so on. This formed the basis for the numbering system on the current bus routes.

The first steam passenger train operated from Dublin to Kingstown (now Dun Laoghaire) on 17 December 1834. It started a fit of 'rail mania', and by the end of 1860, thirty companies operated 1,364 route miles throughout the country using 324 locomotives.

*I*n 1861, various plans were made to link the train termini at Amiens Street (the Great Northern Railway), Kingsbridge (Great Southern and Great Western Railway), Broadstone (Midland Great Western Railway) and Harcourt Street (Dublin, Wicklow and Wexford Railway). It took until 1891 for the controversial Loop Line to be completed, amid many grumbles from Dubliners – the bridge disfigured the city and ruined the view of the Custom House. But at least north and south were finally linked.

*T*he first form of public transport in Dublin was the Ringsend car. Appearing in the seventeenth century, it took passengers from the port to the city centre and was little more than a bench on wheels drawn by a single horse.

The first bus capable of carrying large numbers of passengers at the same time appeared in 1840 and consisted of an enclosed horse-drawn cart carrying ten passengers on the roof and twenty more inside.

In 1872, horse-drawn trams were introduced. These were replaced in 1901 by electrically powered trams, which continued in general use until the last tram in the city left Nelson's Pillar for Dalkey on 10 July 1949.

*B*y the mid-seventeenth century the city was too narrow to cope with the advance in wagons. So in 1667, the Corporation took measures to control hackney taxi coaches in Dublin. The numbers were restricted to thirty, and coach stands were limited to fixed locations: ten in Thomas Street, six in Castle Street, four in Werburgh Street and ten in College Green.

By 1670, people claimed that there were too few taxi coaches, so the number was increased to fifty. In 1703, it went up to 150; in 1732 to 200. By the 1840s, the streets were congested with 1,500 licensed coaches.

By 1904, Dublin was still a city of horses, but the number of cabs had decreased to 656. With drink-driving a major problem, cab drivers were subject to rigorous discipline, and that same year, 1,194 drivers were prosecuted for offences which included 'improperly feeding beast', 'interior of vehicle dirty' and 'not having steps and footboards turned up while disengaged'. Dublin now has over nine thousand licensed taxis.

*I*n 1889, John Boyd Dunlop opened the world's first pneumatic-tyre factory at Upper Stephen's Street. In 1903, the Gordon Bennett Motor Race ushered in the dawn of the motor car in Ireland. Taking place in Athy, County Kildare, the race was famous for being the world's first closed-circuit race, and the cars were weighed in at the Royal Irish Automobile Club on Dawson Street. It made for some spectacle since, at the time, the car population of Ireland was a mere 250. The French were kept informed by James Joyce, reporting on the race for the media in France and drawing on the experience for the short story 'After the Race', which formed part of *Dubliners*.

In 1904, the speed limit in Dublin was twenty m.p.h. But it wasn't until 1909 that the streets of Dublin received their first coating of tar, and cars could at least be assured of a smooth ride. Chaos surely ensued until the first traffic lights in the Republic were installed at the junction of Merrion Square and Clare Street on 27 August 1937.

By the year 2000, car ownership was at 450 cars per 1,000 population, almost the European average.

Alfie Byrne – one of the most famous of Dublin's Lord Mayors and elected ten times since 1930 – was noted for his dapper appearance and his penchant for shaking hands with people. When Henry Ford came to Dublin, he reportedly asked Alfie who he was. 'I'm the man that shook hands with half of Ireland,' replied Alfie. Ford retorted, 'And I'm the man that shook the other half with my Model T motor cars.'

That popular breed, the traffic warden – twenty of them in fact – marched on the streets of Dublin for the first time on 8 October 1968. The first parking meter was installed on Wellington Quay on 14 January 1970, and the price of parking for one hour was a shilling.

By 2003, parking rates had reached €1.90 per hour in the city centre. Failure to pay meant facing the wrath of the dreaded clampers, who were introduced in October 1998 and clamped thirty-eight thousand cars at a charge of €80 each in their first two years of operation. That same year, revenue from parking meters brought in €8.3 million.

The most lucrative street in Dublin for the City Council's clampers is Castle Street – behind City Hall – generating €97,600 in 2002.

WATERWAYS

THE LIFFEY AS IT
STANK LIKE HELL: THE
WATERWAYS OF DUBLIN

At its peak in 1845, the Grand Canal – which was begun in 1755 and reached the Shannon in 1805 – carried an annual load of 110,000 passengers and 310,000 tons of freight. The Royal Canal, which cuts through Dublin's north side, was begun in 1790 and reached the Shannon in 1817. It carried 46,000 passengers and 134,000 tons of freight at its peak in 1833. The Royal Canal closed in 1955 and the Grand Canal in 1960.

The Grand Canal had three uses in its day: to supply the city basin with water; to enable Guinness to transport barrels of porter and stout up the canal to the Midlands; and to supply Guinness's brewery with water for the brewing process. The last Guinness barge to travel the Grand Canal left James's Street Harbour with a cargo for Limerick on 27 May 1960.

The Liffey rises in the Wicklow Mountains and enters Dublin Bay after a journey of 130 kilometres. Ireland's only river to be personified as a female deity, Abhann na Life, an Irish name, was Latinised and appeared on maps into the middle of the nineteenth century as Anna Liffey.

An earlier Irish word for the Liffey is Ruirtheach, meaning turbulent or flooding, but it wasn't until the twentieth century that the danger of flooding was averted by having dams built at Pollaphuca, Golden Falls and Leixlip.

*F*rom Islandbridge to the East Link Toll Bridge, seventeen bridges span the Liffey. The most renowned, the Ha'Penny Bridge, opened in 1816. Officially called Wellington Bridge, after the Battle of Waterloo in 1815 Dubliners called it Cast Iron Bridge, before finally settling on the Ha'Penny Bridge because of the toll of a halfpenny needed to cross it.

Cast in Shropshire, England, and 140 feet long, the bridge replaced a ferry that had previously operated at this point. The turnstiles were removed on 25 March 1919, and crossing from then on was free. The Ha'Penny Bridge was the only pedestrian bridge on the Liffey until the Millennium Bridge was built in 1999.

Although the Ha'Penny Bridge is there to serve the city's pedestrians, they have a green light for only eight seconds on either side to reach the bridge before the trucks resume thundering down the quays.

A plan of the city in 1661 shows just one bridge from the present Church Street. If you needed to cross anywhere downstream, there were a number of ferries that began operating in medieval times. The last ferry – the Ringsend boat – made its final crossing in 1984, when it was made redundant by the opening of the East Link. The ferry was used primarily by dockworkers and local inhabitants up until then.

The latest addition to Dublin's bridges came on 16 June – Bloomsday – 2003 when the James Joyce Bridge was opened, spanning the Liffey between Usher's Island and Ellis Quay. The house at 15 Usher's Island – directly opposite the bridge – was the setting for Joyce's 'The Dead'. But within a few days of the bridge opening, death was the real fear when local children began climbing and sliding on the bridge about twenty-five feet above the traffic. Plans to amend the design were immediately discussed.

Until the East Link Toll Bridge, built in 1984, took some of the pressure off the traffic passing down the quays, a few bizarre proposals were put forward to alleviate the congestion. One suggestion was to widen the road on both sides of the quays, which would have required the demolition of every quayside house and consigned some of Dublin's finest buildings to rubble. Another idea, put forward in 1960 to solve the city's parking problem, involved covering the Liffey to create two huge car parks – from O' Connell Bridge to Butt Bridge on one side and from O'Connell Bridge to the Ha'penny Bridge on the other.

However, for sheer lunacy nothing beats the proposal three years after the Dublin–Kingstown railway opened in 1834. To link the railway to a new line in the south-west, an elevated section of railway from Westland Row (Pearse Station) was to be carried along the south side of Great Brunswick Street (now Pearse Street) to cross D'Olier Street and

Westmoreland Street. With the aid of rows of cast-iron pillars, having one foot in the Liffey and the other on the southern quays, this monstrosity would have gone down as far as the Liffey Valley and through Lucan to serve the south-west area.

There are more than fifty rivers and streams in the Dublin City area, each with its own characteristics and all kept in check by the drainage division of Dublin Corporation. Among the more interesting names of the city's rivers is the palindrome River Camac.

Staring into the murky waters of the Liffey, it is hard to imagine that annually – at the beginning of September – over 250 men, women and children take part in the Liffey Swim. Despite health concerns, the event has taken place since 1924. The race – a mile and a half long – starts from a barge in the river just below Guinness's factory, with the slowest swimmers allowed a handicap. Dublin Fire Brigade is on hand to disinfect the contestants once they've emerged from the river.

Europe's first coordinated lifeboat service was set up in Dun Laoghaire Harbour in about 1800, when lifeboats were organised for Dublin Bay.
However, this was not enough for a Norwegian Captain, Richard

Toutcher, who was the main voice behind a campaign requesting that an 'asylum' harbour for ships waiting to gain entry to Dublin Bay be built as a matter of great urgency. And so, between 1820 and 1827, the east and west piers at Dun Laoghaire were built to enclose an area of water covering 251 acres, making it then the largest man-made harbour in the world.

EYESORES

A POINTLESS POINT:
LANDMARKS THAT LEFT
MORE THAN THEIR
MARK

A building that led to much public derision was the Busáras building, built by Michael Scott of the firm Scott Tallon Walker between 1945 and 1953. The public objected to just about everything – its function, appearance and, in particular, its cost, which came in at a cool £1 million. Had Michael Scott's dream of becoming an actor materialised, then who knows what would be standing on the spot now. Moonlighting under the name Wolf Curran, in 1929 he was performing in a play in London – *The New Gossoon* by George Sheils – to rave reviews, when a *Daily Express* reporter revealed his true identity. He never acted again.

When Dublin Corporation proposed the construction of Civic Offices at Wood Quay, it sparked two decades of widespread protest, as the site lay on the remains of Viking Dublin – the most important discovery of the city's Viking origins ever made.

Designed by Sam Stephenson, phase one required deep foundations for four monolithic towers linked by a glass atrium; the design for phase two was given to Scott Tallon Walker and the building was completed in 1994. Previously, Christ Church was a focal point on the crest of the hill, benefiting from the buildings beneath. With the buildings removed, Christ Church appears dwarfed, isolated and, frankly, quite ordinary.

*L*iberty Hall is probably one of the most unpopular buildings in Dublin, owing mainly to its appearance and also to its prominence. Started in 1961 and finished in 1965, Liberty Hall is sixteen storeys high, making it 195 feet tall. In 1972, a bomb destroyed the magnificent non-reflective glass that was perhaps its only redeeming feature, but sadly for the city the building remained standing. The glass was replaced with the reflective type, which has done nothing but make the building even more garish.

Previously, the building housed a seven-hundred-seat theatre – but with no stage-left entrance. Recently revamped, the theatre now has capacity for 410 people and has stage entrances on both sides.

*T*he greenish building that is the Bank of Ireland on Baggot Street Lower is noteworthy for more than its colour and style. The quantity of bronze manganese used in its construction actually affected the price of bronze manganese on the world market.

*B*ringing tears to the eyes of preservationist Dubliners, demolition began in 1963 on one of the largest expanses of intact Georgian architecture in the world. Sixteen houses on Fitzwilliam Street were destroyed to make way for offices for the semi-state body the Electricity Supply Board.

The imposing but rather uninspiring Wellington Monument in the Phoenix Park was built to commemorate the Duke of Wellington, Arthur Wellesley. Completed in 1861, it is the tallest obelisk in Europe at 205 feet, but it was severely restricted when funds ran dry and plans to erect a statue of Wellington on top of the structure were shelved – which gives the monument little meaning unless one is close enough to read the plaques which were cast from cannons (there was no money for any other metal at the time).

Born in Merrion Street, Dublin, Wellesley was clearly proud of his birthplace when he remarked, 'being born in a stable does not make one a horse'.

The top of Nelson's Pillar, which once dominated O'Connell Street, was blown up by the IRA just before 2 a.m. on 8 March 1966, the year of the fiftieth anniversary of the Easter Rising. The 134 feet and 5 inches tall column had provided a focal point in the street for 157 years, but it was viewed as a symbol of British imperialism rather than the intended nod to Nelson for reopening the sea lanes to mercantile shipping. The battered head of the statue is all that remains; it can be seen in the Civic Museum on South William Street.

The winner of the competition to design a Dublin landmark for the new millennium was Ian Ritchie Architects of London. They came up with 'the

Spire', which pierces the clouds on O'Connell Street. Standing at 120 metres high, constructed of rolled stainless steel sheet and costing tourists a fortune in chiropractors' bills, the Spire was described as follows by Joan O'Connor, chairperson of the judging panel: 'Tangible and enticing at its base, it leads the eye and the imagination upwards, tapering gracefully into an attractively illuminated tip.'

The Spire was erected on 22 January 2003; the light at the top had broken by 3 February. Apart from calling it 'the Spike', Dubliners were quick to offer other suggestions for its title – 'The Why in the Sky', 'The Eyeful Tower', 'The Nail in the Pale' and 'The Pointless Point' among them.

If it wasn't for the intervention in 1986 of An Taisce, the National Trust for Ireland, and Taoiseach Charles Haughey, Temple Bar could now be the greatest carbuncle on the face of the city. The original plans were to construct a huge transportation hub for CIE, the state company responsible for public transport, which would have swallowed up the bulk of the left bank in the city centre.

The carelessness of the plan was revealed in the demolition work, which left thirty-two historical buildings either gutted or demolished by the time an inventory of the architectural heritage had been drawn up. The area was once the nucleus for the city's craftsmen and contained three of Dublin's most famous theatres in the eighteenth century – Smock Alley Theatre, Crow Street Theatre (Theatre Royal) and the

Musick Hall in Fishamble Street. The Musick Hall was where Handel first performed his *Messiah* in April 1742 and caused a storm by donating the proceeds to the Prison Gate Fund and the Prisoners' Dependants.

*D*ue to be completed in 2005, the Dublin Port Tunnel has been a source of both amusement and scorn in the city, with local residents shaken from drilling and traffic to and from the airport being disrupted. However, the farcical news that 157 trucks a day will not be able to use the Dublin Port Tunnel was the final straw. Research by the National Institute of Transport and Logistics indicates that almost 2 per cent of trucks using the port on a daily basis are equal to or above the 4.65-metre height restriction for the Port Tunnel. At a cost of €625 million, it had been hoped that it would take nine thousand heavy goods vehicles a day away from Dublin city centre.

A sixty-metre landmark tower awaits U2 as part of a radical redevelopment of Dublin's docklands. The building, which will be similar in height to Liberty Hall, will be located on Britain Quay – where the River Dodder joins the Liffey – and is to be completed by 2006. The top two floors will be dedicated to a new recording studio for U2, just around the corner from their old premises on Hanover Quay, which the band was unable to save despite a planning battle in 2002.

The 'twisting tower design' (already the minds of Dubliners are plotting a nickname) created by a Dublin-based team, Burdon Dunne and Craig Henry Architects, was chosen from more than five hundred entries from around the world. The fact that it was co-designed by Felim Dunne, a brother-in-law of U2's manager, Paul McGuinness, raised a few eyebrows.

STREET AND PLACE NAMES

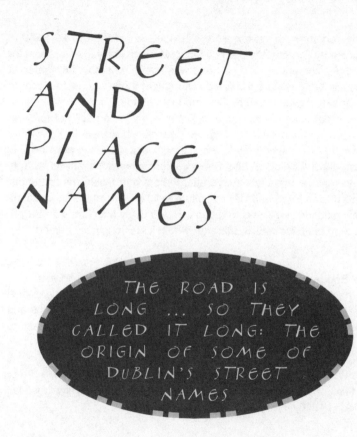

THE ROAD IS LONG ... SO THEY CALLED IT LONG: THE ORIGIN OF SOME OF DUBLIN'S STREET NAMES

After the renaming of Essex Bridge (Capel Street Bridge) in 1874 to honour Henry Grattan, the patriot leader who won legislative freedom for the Irish Parliament in 1782, a trend was begun whereby the names of streets and bridges were renamed in honour of those who were closer to the hearts of the Irish than to the Lord Lieutenants.

Had it not been for the London *Times* – which had still not forgiven Dublin for the demolition of sixteen Georgian buildings in Fitzwilliam Street in 1963 – stating that 'to a conservationist, Dublin is now the City of European Philistinism', the Council might have gone ahead with its plans to rename the city's quays after writers and musicians to honour Dublin's role as European City of Culture in 1991. One of the suggestions – surely made in jest – was to rename Burgh Quay after Chris de Burgh, rather than the Elizabeth Burgh after whom it was originally named.

Carlisle Bridge was built in 1790 and was named after a former Lord Lieutenant of Ireland, the Earl of Carlisle. The original bridge was only forty feet wide and was considered too narrow. It was rebuilt in 1880 and named O'Connell Bridge. At 151 feet, the bridge is as wide as it is long.

The Irish name for The Coombe (An Cum) means a hollow place, a rather dark title for an area that was well known for its maternity hospital, founded in 1826.

*C*romwell's Quarters was quite fittingly known as Murdering Lane until 1876. In 1649, Cromwell lodged nearby at the corner of Werburgh Street and Castle Street, and as with Roundhead Row in the same vicinity, the area was named as part of a themed naming pattern. Roundhead Row was suitably known as Cut-Throat Lane until it was also changed by the Corporation in 1876.

*A*s one of Dublin's newest streets, the unimaginatively named Curved Street doesn't bode well for future street-naming. This is the last link in the pedestrian route from Temple Bar Square to Meeting House Square and is, well, curved. Another Dublin street that suffered in the imagination department is Long Lane, so called because it is … quite long. Not far away is a cul-de-sac off Rathmines Road deceptively named Observatory Lane after Sir Howard Grubb, who invented the periscope for submarines. As for observations, there is little to see there.

*D*errynane Parade is named after the home of Daniel O'Connell in County Kerry, one of a pattern in a naming scheme based on beauty spots in the province of Munster. Others include Glengarriff Parade and Innisfallen Parade – the former called after an area of scenic beauty in County Cork, the latter after an island on the lower lake of Killarney.

*I*f even for a laugh, it's worth mentioning that Frederick Street South was named after Frederick (1705–51), eldest son of George II and the only member of the British Royal Family to be killed by a cricket ball.

Frederick Street North was probably named after Dr Frederick Jebb, Master of the Rotunda Hospital in 1773, whose father was responsible for developing the street.

At the beginning of the twentieth century, Dublin's 'Monto' district was the most notorious red-light district in Europe. Roughly 5,000 soldiers were stationed in the city, which was nicknamed 'the Soldiers Paradise' by the British Army. At its peak, over 1,600 prostitutes plied their trade there, and the area operated until after the British left in 1922.

In a new Ireland, 1925, Frank Duff of the Legion of Mary organised a procession of Legion of Mary girls who blessed every brothel and pinned a picture of Our Lady to the wall. This good deed was bad for the brothels, and they closed soon afterwards. The unfortunate fact was that the area – between Talbot Street and Amiens Street and including Montgomery Street – got its name from Elizabeth Montgomery, the wife of one of Dublin's most prominent property developers, Luke Gardiner. In the eighteenth century, the area had been one of the most highly regarded in Dublin, if not Europe.

Mountjoy Square is the only true square in Dublin, measuring 600 feet in length and 600 feet in width. By comparison, Merrion Square is 1,150 feet long and 650 feet wide.

New Street is actually the oldest street in Dublin, dating back to the thirteenth century and originally part of the Slighe Chualann – one of the four great roads of Ireland that came together in Dublin.

Confiscated in 1560, during the reign of Henry VIII, from the Knights Hospitallers, the Phoenix Park was stocked with deer and opened to the public by the Earl of Chesterfield, viceroy in the 1730s. Chesterfield Avenue, which runs through the park from Kingsbridge to Castleknock, was named after him. He was also responsible for erecting the 'Phoenix' monument, mistakenly believing the park to be named after the mythical bird. The name of the park in fact derives from a spring in the area of the present-day zoo, which was known as Fionn Uisce (clear water). The park covers an area of 1,752 acres and is the largest enclosed park in Europe.

Rialto was the name originally given to Harcourt Bridge over the Grand Canal because of a tenuous resemblance to Rialto Bridge in Venice. The name was later bestowed on the area as a whole, which sadly bears even less of a resemblance to Venice.

Dublin has had its fair share of amusing street names which were thankfully altered through time. Island Street was previously called

Dunghill Lane; Brookfield Avenue – Watery Lane; Lansdowne Road – Watery Lane no. 2; Usher's Lane – Dog and Duck Yard; Belmont Avenue – Coldblow Lane; Cathedral Lane – Cabbage Garden Lane; and finally Mespil Road was known as Gibbet Meadow.

DRINK

HAVE YE NO HOMES
TO GO TO? THE DRINKING
MAN'S CITY

Alcohol has played a prominent role in the history of Dublin. The restorations of two of Dublin's most famous cathedrals – Christ Church and St Patrick's – were paid for by brewing families. In the 1870s, the whiskey distiller Henry Roe paid £230,000 to help restore Christ Church; in the 1860s, Benjamin Guinness paid £160,000 towards the restoration of nearby St Patrick's Cathedral.

By 1660 there were ninety-one breweries and eighteen hundred pubs for four thousand families – one pub to every three citizens in Dublin. By 1633 the entire area beneath Christ Church scandalously housed a succession of taverns, in a locale that saw buildings accommodating the law courts erected against the cathedral walls. Known as 'Hell', this arched, gloomy area lay about ten feet below the level of the present cathedral's floor. Apartments for single men in the seedy district were advertised as, 'To be let, furnished apartments in hell. N.B. They are well suited to a lawyer.'

A threatened strike in 1963 by Dublin barmen who refused to serve 'heavy' meals, only soup and sandwiches, was thankfully avoided. But the longest strike in Ireland began in Downey's pub, on the corner of Marine Road and George's Street, Dun Laoghaire, on 5 March 1939, and it ended in May 1953 on the death of the pub owner. The strike was over wage increases and union representation. And apart from participating in the longest strike, the union involved also holds the title for the longest abbreviated name in Irish trade history – the INUVG&ATA (Irish National Union of Vintners, Grocers & Allied Trade Assistants). The pub was later demolished to make way for Dun Laoghaire Shopping Centre, but its taps can still be seen in the Stillorgan Orchard pub.

After founding his own brewery in Leixlip, Arthur Guinness moved to Dublin in 1759 and signed a nine-thousand-year lease on St James's Gate for an annual rent of £45. Guinness's brewery was founded in 1759 and covers over sixty-four acres.

Arthur Guinness's opposition to the United Irishmen – which led to the drink being nicknamed 'Guinness's black Protestant porter' – together with the threat of a popular boycott, inspired the start of an export business in 1796. The initial shipment to England was a humble six and a half barrels. Today, Guinness sells ten million pints a day in 150 countries.

Guinness formally adopted the harp as its symbol on 5 April 1962.

Father Theobald Mathew held a temperance meeting behind the Custom House in 1840. By the end of the day, almost five thousand people had taken the pledge, a figure that grew to almost a hundred thousand by the time the year was out, possibly encouraged by the medal presented to each person.

Thankfully for the brewers, few kept the pledge. Father Mathew was later arrested because he was unable to pay for all the medals, and he lost the chance to become Bishop of Cork.

Carmelite Father John Spratt of Whitefriars Street Priory toiled endlessly with Father Mathew to make the country dry. He argued that if people had things to do on Sunday, they wouldn't drink so much, and he pushed for the zoo to open on Sunday – which it did, with an entrance fee of one penny.

Mother Redcap's pub on Christ Church Back Lane was originally established in 1760, reopening in its present form in 1988. Its name came from Old Mother Redcap who ran a brothel there in the eighteenth century. Its chequered past did not prevent it from winning a Good Pub Guide award in 1992.

A sign outside the Brazen Head pub on 20 Lower Bridge Street boasts that it was founded in 1198, which would make it the oldest pub in Dublin. However, this date refers to a tavern built on the same site, with the present building dating to only 1710. Technically, therefore, the oldest pub in Dublin is the Boot Inn at Cloghran, near Dublin airport, which dates from 1593.

What both pubs have in common, however, are homages to Robert Emmet, the main strategist of the 1803 Rising. The Boot Inn has a portrait of Emmet, footnoted with a poetic tribute from his childhood companion Thomas Moore. Emmet also kept a room at the Brazen Head, and his famous speech from the dock is displayed in full on the walls within.

Anyone familiar with Dublin pub lore will be well aware of the reputation of McDaid's pub on Harry Street. Brendan Behan offered to paint the toilets for the price of a pint and took over a corner of the bar, where he sat with his typewriter and wrote while he drank and goaded poet Patrick Kavanagh.

The pub went up for sale in 1972, and a British lady who wanted to add a literary pub to her growing list outbid barman of thirty-five years, Paddy O'Brien, at the auction. Offered a job managing Grogan's pub on South William Street, O'Brien left, and in what became known as 'the flight of the faithful', all the regular McDaid's customers followed him. Behan and Kavanagh were dead by then, but many who took their places at the bar – Anthony Cronin and Liam O'Flaherty included – brought their 'spirits' with them.

The International Bar on Wicklow Street was converted from a hostel in 1886 and has changed very little since. Its main claim to fame is the rowdy comedy nights hosted in the cellar below, a venue where *Father Ted*'s Ardal O'Hanlon cut his teeth for a weekly wage of £12 in 1988.

Mulligan's pub on Poolbeg Street is almost an institution. JFK frequented the pub when he worked as European reporter for the Hearst newspaper dynasty in 1945.

Stools and chairs were once banned because the proprietor at the time, James Mulligan, believed real men should stand while they drank. To ensure that drinking is all customers can do, no food is served there apart from the occasional peanut or crisp.

Claiming to be the longest pub in Europe, the exterior of The Hole in the Wall on Blackhorse Avenue on the north side of the city measures 330 feet. Established in 1681, it's also one of the oldest pubs in Dublin. The name of the pub comes from a hole in its wall that soldiers stationed in nearby Phoenix Park could order drink through, thus avoiding breaching regulations by being in a licensed premises while on duty.

Patrick Conway's pub on Parnell Street was first licensed in 1745, making it the oldest pub in the north of the city. It was outside this pub that Patrick Pearse, president of the provisional government of the Irish Republic of 1916 and commandant-general of its forces during the 1916 Rising, was wounded in the fighting and surrendered. A plaque commemorating this event was unveiled outside the bar in 1995.

Ryan's of Parkgate Street, built in the 1840s, is a fine example of a Victorian pub. On St Patrick's Day, 1999, fourteen US radio stations phoned there to create live link-ups with Irish expatriates in the US.

Davy Byrne's pub on Duke Street underwent a considerable facelift in 1941, the year James Joyce died. Since this was one of Joyce's favourite haunts, it was probably wise to wait until the great writer had passed on, as the refurbishment transformed the bar dramatically.

Every year on 16 June, Bloomsday, Joyce buffs meet here and order the meal that Leopold Bloom had on that day as depicted in *Ulysses*: a gorgonzola cheese sandwich with mustard and a glass of burgundy.

The Duke pub on Duke Street, established in 1822, displays several letters from James Joyce on its walls. In one letter to T. S. Eliot after the death of Joyce's father, Joyce expresses guilt that he had never returned to Ireland to see him, despite promises that he would. In another, sent to Joyce's patron Harriet Shaw Weaver, Joyce mentions that a 'family fire brigade' had rescued the charred remains of *Ulysses* after a fit of anger over its initial reception had made him discard it.

In 1818, a fire in a troop billet that had previously been home to the Earl of Shelbourne led to the rebuilding and founding of the Shelbourne Hotel in 1824. The Constitution of the Irish Free State was drafted here; Graham Greene wrote part of *The End of the Affair* in one of its rooms. Other past guests include Rock Hudson, Montgomery Clift and John Huston. Peter O'Toole stayed there while appearing in *Waiting for Godot* at the Abbey in the early 1970s and is said to have bathed in a tub filled with twenty-four magnums of champagne. Before the outbreak of World War I, Alois Hitler, Adolf Hitler's half-brother, worked in the Shelbourne as a wine waiter.

O'Donoghue's pub on Merrion Row was a grocer's and wine-and-spirit merchant's when it was built in 1789, before officially becoming O'Donoghue's in 1934 and introducing traditional music, for which it is now legendary. One of the first bars to pick up on the ballad boom in the 1960s, it was virtually a home away from home for the famous musicians The Dubliners. Christy Moore, Phil Lynott, The Fureys and Paul Brady all appeared there in that same decade.

Kavanagh's pub on Prospect Square, also known as the Gravediggers' because of its proximity to Prospect Cemetery, Glasnevin, was first managed by John Kavanagh who had twenty-five children, three of whom went to fight in the American Civil War. It has since remained in the same family for six generations.

Built in 1798, Johnnie Fox's in the Dublin Mountains is the highest pub in the country at a thousand feet above sea level. The pub is known for its entertainment. On New Year's Day 1995, Elvis impersonator John Reid collapsed after a show here. He died seven days later on 8 January, Elvis' birthday.

ARTS AND CULTURE

IS THAT A CONDOM
I SEE BEFORE ME?
CENSORSHIP, THE ARTS
AND BONO'S VOX

Home of the Dublin Total Abstinence Society until 1872 and the City Morgue until 1903, the Abbey Theatre opened on 27 December 1904. Unfortunately, it burned down on 17 July 1951. The play that evening closed with soldiers on stage singing 'Keep the Home Fires Burning', from Sean O'Casey's *The Plough and the Stars.*

The new building, built in the 1960s and designed by Michael Scott, houses two theatres – the Abbey and the smaller Peacock. Aesthetically disappointing – at least from the exterior, as the building presents itself as a huge wall of grey brick – conspiracies for another fire have been a constant rumour since its completion, and it is likely that the theatre will move to O'Connell Street.

On 1 July 1871, Lord Mayor John Campbell JP laid the foundation stone for one of Dublin's most popular entertainment venues, the Gaiety Theatre. A shining example of what can be achieved in a short space of time, the building was completed in only six months, with workmen toiling through the night by torchlight. The first performance on opening night, 27 November 1871, was Oliver Goldsmith's *She Stoops to Conquer.*

In 1957, Dublin staged an international theatre festival with one of the plays, *The Rose Tattoo* by Tennessee Williams, causing a huge amount of controversy. Alan Simpson, the producer, was arrested for staging an 'indecent' performance – specifically, this referred to a scene where a character was alleged to have dropped a condom on the floor. The court proceedings went on for a year, and although the judge threw out the case, the Pike Theatre – co-founded by Simpson in 1953 and famous for bringing Beckett's *Waiting for Godot* to Dublin that same year – never recovered.

In 1932, the first Irish film censor, James Montgomery, was appointed and stated that he wanted to protect Irish audiences from the 'Californication' of American films. He also referred to the Gate and Abbey theatres as 'Sodom and Begorrah'.

The 'official printer to his Majesty in Ireland', Humphrey Powell, was given a special grant to establish the first printing press in Ireland, and *The Book of Common Prayer,* the first book to be produced in Ireland, was printed in Dublin in 1551.

The first book printed in the Irish language was John Kearney's *Aibidil Gaoidheilge agus Caiticiosma* (*A Gaelic Alphabet and Catechism*), printed in Dublin in 1571 by John Ussher. Usher's Quay is named after his family.

In 1698, because it advocated Irish autonomy, the first Irish book to be burned was *The Case of Ireland Stated* by William Molyneux.

The first newspaper in Dublin came out in 1685 and was called *The Dublin Newsletter*. Printed three times a week, it lasted only seven months.

During the first half of the eighteenth century, 165 newspapers were started in Dublin. Few regarded advertising as important and thus were gone in a matter of months.

At the beginning of the twentieth century, the *United Irishman* newspaper was a staunch warden of moral values. Even the mutoscope machines – the predecessors to the cinema, where one inserted a coin, turned a handle and viewed a series of images at high speed – at the Royal Dublin Society's Spring Show in 1904 managed to incur its wrath. The titles of the movies on show that year were indeed devious: 'Mixed Bathing', 'How Minnie Got Her Leg Pulled', 'Married Women Will Appreciate This', 'Changing the Bather's Clothes' and 'The Lovers Were Having a Good Time but the Wife Came on the Scene' were among the more outrageous that the *United Irishman* chastised.

The first custom-built cinema in Ireland, The Volta, opened in Dublin on 20 December 1909. The manager was James Joyce.

The Savoy Cinema, Dublin, was opened by W. T. Cosgrave on 29 November 1929. The first showing was *Ireland, a Government Documentary*.

The Adelphi Cinema opened on 12 January 1939 and during its time played host to the only Dublin appearance by the Beatles, on 7 November 1963, and to Bob Dylan, Louis Armstrong, Ella Fitzgerald, Marlene Dietrich, Roy Orbison, Gene Pitney and Diana Ross. The cinema closed in 1995.

The greatest rumpus caused at a Dublin cinema was courtesy of one of the original boy bands, the Bay City Rollers. Eight gardaí and 150 fans were injured when rioting broke out on 22 April 1975 at the old Star Cinema, Crumlin during a performance.

Richard Poekrich, the Monaghan-born man who spent most of his time in Dublin, first introduced his bizarre musical instrument to a Dublin audience in 1743. The 'glasspiel' or 'verillion' was actually eighteen glasses filled with varying quantities of water, all placed on a cloth-covered table. His simple method of resonating the glasses with his fingertips to produce a musical note was improved upon by Benjamin Franklin. Both Mozart and Beethoven wrote music for it, and with water no longer necessary it became known as the 'armonica'.

The Oscar statuette was designed by a Dublin-born art director, Cedric Gibbons. In 1924, he began his thirty-two-year stint as supervising art director for some fifteen hundred MGM films. Apart from designing the Oscar statuette, he won it eleven of the thirty-seven times he was nominated.

When the codicil to the will of Hugh Lane, a patron of the arts who was killed in the sinking of the *Lusitania* in 1915, was not witnessed, a long and bitter squabble began between the British and Irish authorities over the legacy of his vast art collection. The dispute concerned Lane's anger over Dublin Corporation's refusal to house the collection in a specially built gallery and so bequeathing his collection to the National Gallery of London in an earlier will.

In 1959, it was decided to divide the collection and alternate the exhibition in five-year cycles. Corot, Degas, Manet, Monet, Pissarro, Renoir and others now spend their time between London and Dublin's Hugh Lane Municipal Gallery of Modern Art.

In 1986, on Beckett's eightieth birthday, a gold *torc* presented by Taoiseach Garret FitzGerald was accepted by the writer's niece on her uncle's behalf. In Celtic culture, the most important people were the *brehona* (judges) and the *filí* (poets). The gold *torc* is the symbol of the position of *saoí*, which is the highest Celtic honour that can be bestowed.

A graduate of Trinity College, Beckett famously said of the place, 'Dublin University contains the cream of Ireland: rich and thick.'

U2 fans could spend a week in Dublin place-spotting. The East Link Bridge is featured in the first 'Pride' video, directed by Donald Cammell; the

Grand Canal Docks are where the cover picture of *October* was shot; Ballymun, the unsuccessful and rather bleak housing project in the north of Dublin, less than a mile from Bono's childhood home, contains the seven towers Bono was referring to in the song 'Running To Stand Still'; the Bonavox hearing-aid shop on North Earl Street provided the inspiration for the teenage Paul Hewson's moniker.

One of the places U2 played live during their early days, the Dandelion Market, is now the location of the St Stephen's Green Shopping Centre; the Baggot Inn is another place U2 played when the band were starting out – it closed down temporarily in the mid-nineties and was purchased by a consortium including former Ireland football-manager Jack Charlton.

JOYCE'S
DUBLIN

DUNGBIN: JAMES JOYCE'S
FAIR CITY

*F*or James Joyce, nothing was trivial and almost everything had its cosmic significance. He was born on 2 February 1882, auspicious in his eyes because it was the same year that de Valera was born. One wonders then what he made of the place he was born – 41 Brighton Square, Rathgar, Dublin. Brighton Square is not a square at all but a triangle.

*A*part from his literary genius, Joyce was also a singer of some renown, appearing on the same platform as tenor John McCormack and coming second in one of Dublin's premier singing contests, the Feis Ceoil, on 16 May 1904, missing out on first place because of his refusal to sing a piece at sight. He threw the medal in the Liffey, however, being both disgusted at losing and sore at not being able to pawn the medal.

In Dublin at the beginning of the twentieth century, pawning was a regular weekly event for much of the city's populace. In 1904, it was found that 2,866,084 pawn tickets had been issued, representing loans of £547,453.

*T*he Martello Tower in Sandycove – a bohemian residence where Joyce himself lodged between 9 and 14 September 1904 with Oliver St John Gogarty (the model for Buck Mulligan) and Chenevix Trench (Haines) – is where *Ulysses* opens. During the night of 14 September, Trench had a nightmare and fired a revolver that almost killed Joyce, who left immediately and never returned.

Joyce buffs will spend aeons arguing whether Joyce was destined to lodge there because, curiously enough, the centenary celebration of Bloomsday on 16 June 2004 coincides with the bi-centenary celebration of the Martello Tower, as the order to build the tower was dated 16 June 1804.

A set of fourteen bronze plaques set into the pavements of Dublin's streets loosely follows the route taken by Leopold Bloom, the central character in *Ulysses*. Starting at Middle Abbey Street, the route ends at the National Museum, and each plaque has a quote from the eighth section of the book. The project was sponsored by the drinks company Cantrell & Cochrane, and the sculptor was Robin Buick.

One of the few remaining literary landmarks associated with James Joyce was restored to its former glory in January 2004: 15 Usher's Island, the 'dark, gaunt house' on the south quays of Dublin's River Liffey, immortalised in Joyce's best-known short story 'The Dead', just about escaped the wrecking ball.

When Dublin barrister and Joyce enthusiast Brendan Kilty bought the four-storey Georgian building in 2001, it was little more than a shell. The top floor had been torn down to save its then owners the trouble of patching up a leaking roof, the back wall was buckled to the point of near collapse and Brendan Kilty personally gathered two buckets of syringes from the ground floor of what had become a squat. Before being listed for preservation, the house had been earmarked for demolition to make way for the James Joyce Bridge across the Liffey.

Apart from being the location of Joyce's short story, it was here that he had dinner with his family each year on 6 January to celebrate the Feast of the Epiphany, dining on a Christmas goose. The house belonged to his aunts, and he drew on his memories of it when he was writing the story.

Some of the names Joyce uses for Dublin in *Finnegans Wake* are: Doubtlynn, Drooplin, Dabblin, Dumplan, Dungbin, Dyoublong, Dirt Dump, dub him Lynn, Londub, Dumpling and nill, Budd!

When Joyce first chanced upon Nora Barnacle, his future wife, on 10 June 1904 on Dublin's Nassau Street, Nora was working as a chambermaid in Finn's Hotel on South Leinster Street. She came from Galway. Joyce's father, upon hearing her surname, exclaimed, 'Jaysus, I suppose she'll stick to him anyway.'

The character Leopold Bloom was based on a Good Samaritan who came to Joyce's aid after he had made advances on a girl he thought was alone. When he received a bloody nose, courtesy of the lady's partner, a passing gentleman, a Dublin Jew by the name of Alfred Hunter, helped him out.

As an advertising canvasser, Bloom often pondered the unexplored possibilities of the art of advertising. Little wonder when the type of ads that appeared in Dublin at the time were of the kind displayed in the *Leader* by a publican named McGrath:

> MY ALES AND MY BRANDIES
> MY WINE AND MY RUMS,
> ARE THE FINEST WITH WHICH
> MEN COULD MOISTEN THEIR GUMS.

Joyce's obsession with accuracy and detail in his writing led him to alter a passage in the 'Wandering Rocks' section, chapter 10, in *Ulysses* that referred to a tree on Charleville Mall as an elm when it should have been a poplar.

However, his brag that if Dublin were to be destroyed by a bomb it could be rebuilt brick by brick using *Ulysses* as a template fails – he places the Brazen Head pub in Winetavern Street, when it is in fact on nearby Lower Bridge Street.

SHOPS

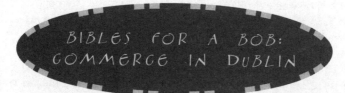

BIBLES FOR A BOB:
COMMERCE IN DUBLIN

The first shop in Dublin to put its name over the door in Irish was Cathal Mac Garvey's tobacco shop 'An Stad' in North Frederick Street. He was fined five shillings for breaking the law, but the name remained.

Said to be the oldest shop in Dublin, the premises of Thomas Read, cutler, were originally built in the 1670s but were relocated to 4 Parliament Street when this street was built by the Wide Streets Commissioners in the 1760s.

Among the fascinating items in Read's shop were the world's smallest pair of scissors, which were said to be able to cut a 'housefly's whiskers', and the world's largest penknife, with 576 blades. In 1821, the business received a Royal Charter to make needles for the British forces.

The shop was eventually purchased and converted to a pub in 1989, when John Read Cowle ended a family association that had lasted for over three hundred years.

The 1917 Chamber of Commerce guide lists over three hundred items made in Dublin at the time, ranging from account books to gunpowder, periscopes and 'Irish curled hair'. It also noted that a Dublin firm was the first manufacturer of soda water.

*T*he honour of opening the world's first purpose-built department store goes to Dublin. Peter Paul McSwiney and George Delaney opened their Palatial Mart on Sackville Street (now O'Connell Street) in 1853. Today the store is known as Clery and Company.

*O*n 25 October 1854 at the Battle of Balaclava, during the Crimean War, a bugle sounded the charge of what became known as one of the most disastrous attacks in British war history – the Charge of the Light Brigade. Perhaps the brigade were unaware that the curse of the Irish – rather than the luck – was with them, since the bugle used to sound the charge was fashioned in McNeill's Music Shop in Capel Street, founded in 1834.

*T*he Ha'penny Bridge and its vicinity was a popular place of trade in the mid-twentieth century. One trader, Joe Clarke, sold books, which included special offers of 'bibles for a bob'. When asked by one customer whether they were Catholic or Protestant bibles, Joe answered, 'They're God's bibles, sir, and I think he was a Jew.'

*S*hoemakers in Dublin in the mid-twentieth century did everything to encourage people to buy their wares, with signs on the window ranging from the poetic – 'Don't pass this shop/And have that feel/That you are down on the heel' – to ones capitalising on people's health fears – 'We sole the living not the dead. Don't risk cold and flu, get leather on your shoe.'

Dublin writer and chronicler Eamonn Mac Thomais recalls visiting a 'his 'n' hers' hair studio in the 1970s and asking the woman attending him if she could trim his beard.

'Oh Janey,' she replied, 'I never trimmed a beard, mister.'

'Lucy, Lucy,' she called to another woman, 'do you know anything about trimming beards?'

'No, Jacintha,' replied Lucy, 'but I suppose it's the same as cutting heads only it's upside down.'

CHARACTERS

BUGLER DUNNE AND
NANCY NEEDLEBALLS:
THE CHARMERS ON
DUBLIN'S STREETS

In mid-twentieth-century Dublin, Thompson's Bakery in Bridgefoot Street not only baked bread but also provided heat for the city's homeless. Famous Dublin characters such as Johnny Forty Coats, Damn the Weather, Hairy Yank, Shell Shock Joe, Bugler Dunne and Bang Bang Dudley, who shot people on trams with his imaginary gun, congregated at the 'hot wall', where the bread was baked inside and heated those standing outside.

Hairy Yank bragged that he was a millionaire who had lost all his money in the Wall Street Crash of 1929. Whether or not there was any truth in the rumour is anyone's guess, but he was a good schemer nevertheless. He returned to Dublin and sold cabbage plants for the vegetable patches in women's gardens, operating on one street at a time. Once the plants were sold and planted, he'd return at night to dig them up and resell them to the innocent housewives on another street.

Damn the Weather was a character who wore a long, black coat and an open-neck shirt and damned the weather with his incessant rhyme:

SUMMER'S TOO BLOODY HOT,
WINTER'S TOO BLOODY COLD,
SPRING IS ONLY FOR LAMBS

AND AUTUMN FOR CLEANING TREES.
OH, DAMN THE WEATHER.

Since he wore the same clothes all the time, he possibly damned the summer more than the winter.

A lthough it became a common moniker for a homeless down and out, there was a Johnny Forty Coats and his real name was Jack Russell, an only child whose father died when he was sixteen. The story goes that his mother took up with another man, and Jack hit the streets. His life was spent rambling the area between Bridgefoot Street and Francis' Corner, and he lived in a coal shed in The Coombe.

B ugler Dunne wasn't a bugler at all, but his father had been and Dunne wore his red coat replete with medals. Dunne's story was that his father was the bugler at the Battle of Balaclava where the Light Brigade made its ill-fated charge. His claim was that as they were riding into the valley he was asked to sound the retreat but got confused, blowing for an advance charge instead.

O f the female characters that roamed Dublin's streets, the more renowned were All Parcels, who collected waste paper, Nancy Needleballs and

Lavender Woman, who sold sprigs of lavender with the catch cry, 'Lavender for your drawers, mam. It will keep them cool in this sticky weather.'

DUBLIN'S COMMUNITIES

THEY CAME, THEY SAW, SOME CONQUERED: IMMIGRANTS WHO MADE DUBLIN THEIR HOME

*I*mmigrants who left their mark on Dublin include the Huguenots (French Calvinist Protestants) who arrived in Dublin in the seventeenth century after persecutions in France. Among them was Jeremiah D'Olier, goldsmith, City Sheriff and a founder of the Bank of Ireland. D'Olier Street was named after him. Other famous Huguenots were David La Touche, banker; John Rocque, cartographer (Rocque's map); James Gandon and Richard Cassels, architects; Joseph Sheridan Le Fanu, novelist; and William Dargan, railway pioneer.

*T*he Religious Society of Friends, or Quakers, whose first meeting house was built in Sycamore Alley in 1692, began to acquire many properties in the eighteenth century. The congregation contributed many family-business names: Thomas Weir, jewellers; John Johnston, of Johnston, Mooney and O'Brien bakers; Thomas Heiton, coal merchants; Alex Findlater, wine merchant; and, perhaps the most well known, Joshua Bewley, who began his tea and coffee business in 1840.

*T*he first Jewish community settled in Dublin over three hundred years ago, opening a synagogue in Temple Bar's Crane Lane. Some were of Spanish and Portuguese origin, and many more fled the pogroms in Russia in the late nineteenth century. An area around the South Circular Road became known as Little Jerusalem, and two former Lord Mayors of

Dublin were both Jewish and related – Robert Briscoe, 1956/7, and his son, Ben, 1961/2.

*I*van Beshoff, the Russian mutineer believed to be the last survivor of the crew of the battleship *Potemkin*, died on 25 October 1987. Bad food was the main cause of the famous mutiny in 1905. However, Dubliners didn't object when Beshoff came to Ireland and opened the now famous fish-and-chip shop, Beshoff's.

EVENTS

FOR THE RECORD:
SOME ODDBALL
ACHIEVEMENTS

Dubliner Patrick Breadan enlisted in the RAF at seventeen and, with a shamrock-emblazoned Spitfire, became the fourth highest air ace of World War II.

The first Irish person to achieve flight was Richard Crosbie, who ascended from Ranelagh Gardens in a balloon on 19 July 1785 and made it as far as the North Strand.

In the summer of 1919, the Britons John Alcock and Arthur Brown made the first non-stop Atlantic crossing, from Newfoundland to Connemara.

The greater challenge of going against the wind, from east to west, was not attained until 12 April 1928, when the *Bremen* took off from Baldonnel, County Dublin, captained by Colonel James Fitzmaurice.

Although technically he never completed it, Robert Loraine made what is recognised as the first successful aeroplane flight across the Irish Sea, from Holyhead to Howth, on 11 September 1910. His engine cut out six times during the crossing, and he landed in the sea a few hundred metres short of the Irish coast.

The first successful flight across the Irish Sea was by Mr Windham Sadler, who flew from Dublin to Anglesey by balloon in 1817.

In the 1913 *Daily Mail* Hydro-Aeroplane Trial for seaplanes, the aim being to fly 1,540 miles around the UK, there was only one contestant.

The sole entrant was Harry Hawker, and he came down near Dublin. He received a consolation prize of £1,000.

Croke Park, the headquarters of the Gaelic Athletic Association (GAA), is the fourth largest stadium in Europe after the Nou Camp in Barcelona, the Bernabeu in Madrid and the San Siro in Milan.

Since its construction in the 1920s, it had consisted of three stands (the Hogan Stand, the Cusack Stand and the Nally Stand) and two standing areas – the Canal End and a terrace known as Hill 16, which was constructed from the rubble left in Sackville Street (O'Connell Street) after the 1916 Rising. Redevelopment, which ended in the demolition of Hill 16 in November 2003, increased the capacity of the stadium to 82,300. The site was originally owned by Maurice Butterly in the 1870s and was known as the City and Suburban Racecourse. The GAA became one of the ground's more frequent users, and in 1908 Frank Dineen purchased the fourteen-acre site for the sum of £3,250. Five years later, the GAA bought the site from Frank Dineen for £3,500 and renamed the ground Croke Park in honour of the association's first patron, Archbishop Croke of Cashel.

Many football supporters argue that the Shamrock Rovers team of the 1920s was the best ever. Around this time emerged the famous forward line known as the 'Four Fs' – Bob Fulham, John Joe Flood, 'Kruber' Fagan and Billy Farrell.

Bob Fulham scored Ireland's first international goal, against Italy, on 23 April 1927. John Joe Flood scored three of Ireland's four goals against Belgium on 20 April 1929, making Ireland's first international hat trick.

On 26 September 1957, Shamrock Rovers became the first League of Ireland team to play in the European Cup. Unfortunately, they lost 6–0 to Manchester United.

The first rugby match in Dublin was against England in 1875 and took place at the Leinster Cricket Ground, Rathmines, since Lansdowne Road, home of the Irish Rugby Football Union since 1873, was deemed to be inadequate for a rugby match at the time. England won. With a year to improve things, the first international rugby match at Lansdowne Road was played on 16 December 1876. England won again.

FREEMEN

LAND OF THE FREE:
PEOPLE WHO RECEIVED
THE HONORARY FREEDOM
OF DUBLIN

As the highest award in the city's gift, the Honorary Freedom of Dublin is awarded very rarely, and in its 124-year history it has been conferred on only seventy people, including Pope John Paul II; theatrical personalities Noel Purcell and Maureen Potter; the Crown Prince and Princess of Japan, now Emperor Akihito and Empress Michiko; Nelson Mandela, who received the Honorary Freedom in 1988 while he was still a political prisoner and did not sign the roll until after his release from captivity in 1990; and the four members of U2.

For a city that has always prided itself on its interest in sport, the Honorary Freedom has been conferred on only two sporting heroes: cyclist Stephen Roche, winner of the Giro d'Italia, the Tour de France and the World Cycling Championship, in 1987; and Jack Charlton, manager of the Republic of Ireland football team, in 1994.

The Roll of Honorary Freedom has travelled outside Ireland only once. In 1946, the playwright and Nobel laureate George Bernard Shaw was awarded the freedom of his native city of Dublin. However, at ninety, Shaw was too infirm to travel to his birthplace for the conferring ceremony, and instead the Dublin city manager, P. J. Hernon, went to Shaw's home at Ayot St Lawrence in England where Shaw signed the Freedom Roll on 28 August 1946.

The Honorary Freedom of Dublin has been awarded to only five women: Margaret, Lady Sandhurst in 1889, for her services to charity; Maureen Potter in 1984, for her services to Dublin theatre; the Crown Princess of Japan in 1985, to mark closer trade links between Ireland and Japan; Mother Teresa of Calcutta in 1993; and Burmese pro-democracy leader Aung San Suu Kyi on 1 November 1999, who was unable to sign the role since she was under house arrest.

The Freedom of the City of Dublin has been awarded to three Presidents of the United States: General Ulysses S. Grant on 30 December 1878; John Fitzgerald Kennedy on 28 June 1963, during his famous visit to Ireland five months before his assassination in Dallas; and William Jefferson Clinton on 1 December 1995 at a public ceremony in College Green, during his first visit to Ireland to promote the Northern peace process.

ACKNOWLEDGEMENTS

Many thanks to Jonathan Williams, who helped me with this project and who was a great source of advice throughout the book's production. To all at New Island, in particular to Emma Dunne the editor, many thanks for all your assistance. To Barry Keane: thanks a lot for reading this and a scatter of other items over the years. To Tom Mathews – love the cartoons. To Andrew and Jack at the *In Dublin* office for holding the fort while I skived off to research this book, and to past *In Dublin* editors Declan and Alana for giving a struggling writer a hand, cheers guys! Finally to Mum, Dad and my very patient wife, Asha: all your wonderful support is never forgotten.

I am also indebted to the following authors whose work was particularly helpful: Douglas Bennett, J. Brady, Peter Costello, Ken Finlay, Pat Liddy, Colm Lincoln, John McCormack, Frank McDonald, Eamonn Mac Thomais, Aubrey Malone, Desmond Moore, E.E. O'Donnell, John O'Donovan and Peter Pearson.